A simple book of affirmations through the spirit of seeds.

I
am
QUINOA!

Written and illustrated by
Apple Resonance

LemongrassPress.com

Text, illustrations and book design: Apple Resonance
Editor: Chi Balmaceda-Gutierrez
Photo credits: Apple Resonance

Printed in The USA
Published by Lemongrass Press.
All rights reserved.

Our mission at Lemongrass Press is to promote well-being, good values, self-awareness, self-reliance, environmental consciousness, nature stewardship and regenerative conservation through gardening, seed-saving and growing our own food.

For more information, send your inquiries to
info@lemongrasspress.com
Lemongrass Press, USA

10 9 8 7 6 5 4 3 2 1

We **GROW** books inspired by Life in *Nature*.

www. LemongrassPress.com

This book is dedicated:

To my son, Michael.

To my baby, Anastasya Mikaela.

To all the Starseeds.

To all the Indigo, Crystal and Rainbow children of the Earth.

To all the stewards and co-creators of Mother Nature.

Always thankful and grateful

My sincerest acknowledgements and gratitude to all the special people who I consider as important ingredients in the creation of this vision.

Monsieur Dominic Sennelier
Pang Sharman
Quin Shakra

Julie Bushini and Kaia Streb
Niel Paulsen and Michael Mitton
of The Findhorn Foundation
Chi Balmaceda Guttierrez
and my father, Carmelo Antonio Chan.

Whether you tend a garden or not,

YOU are the gardener of your own **BEING**,

The **SEED** of your **DESTINY**.

- The Findhorn Foundation

I

am not a . . . .

Lima!

I

am not a . . . .

Fava!

I
am
not
a
CHIA.

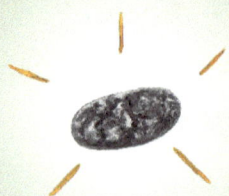

I
am
a

QUINOA!

Are You a...

Lima?

Are You a... Fava?

Are

You

a...

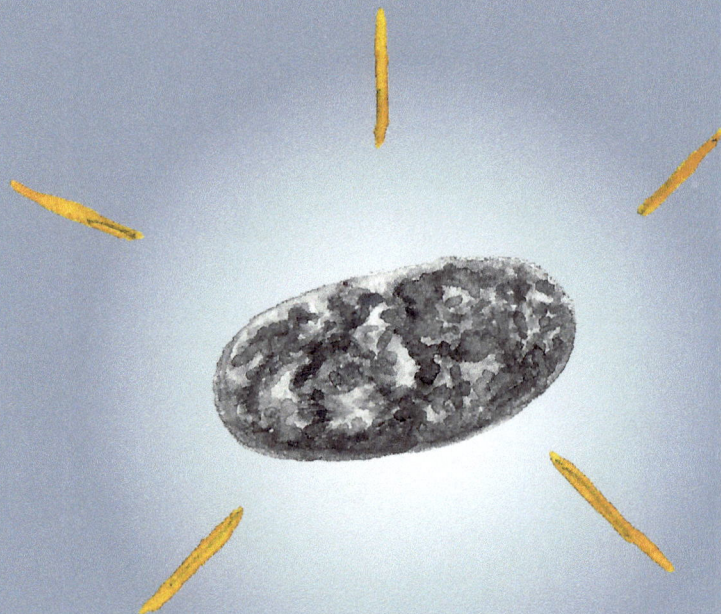

CHIA?

Are

Y
O
U

a...

QUINOA?

You
can be a...

Lima!

You
can be a...

Fava!

can be a... YOU

QUINOA!

I
am
a

SEED.

You

are

a

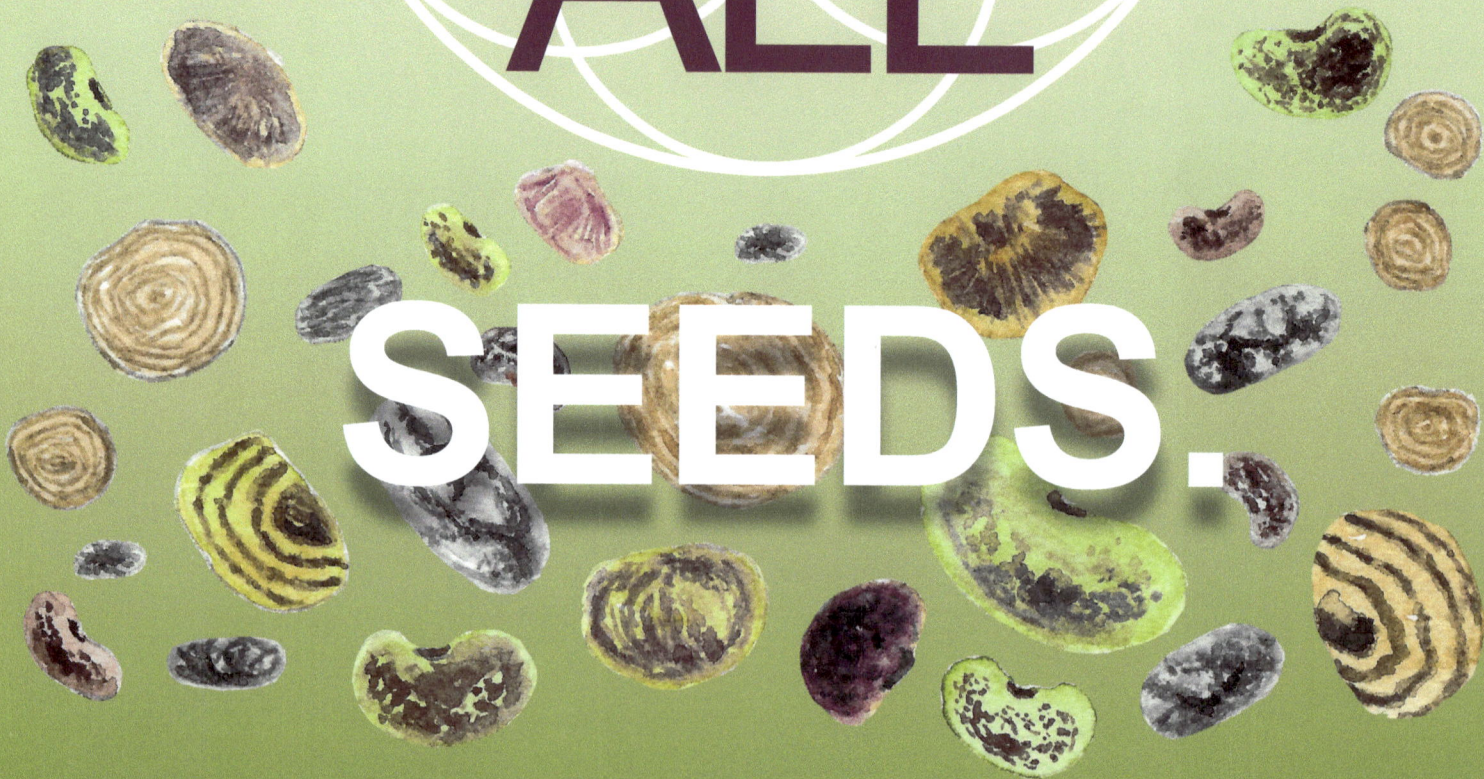

With a **PURPOSE** to **GROW,**

and spread GOOD DEEDS!

Who
YOU
are,

and who you are

NOT...

It is

GOOD
to
KNOW.

Truly
finding
oneself,

is not that
easy.

WE ALL
KNOW.

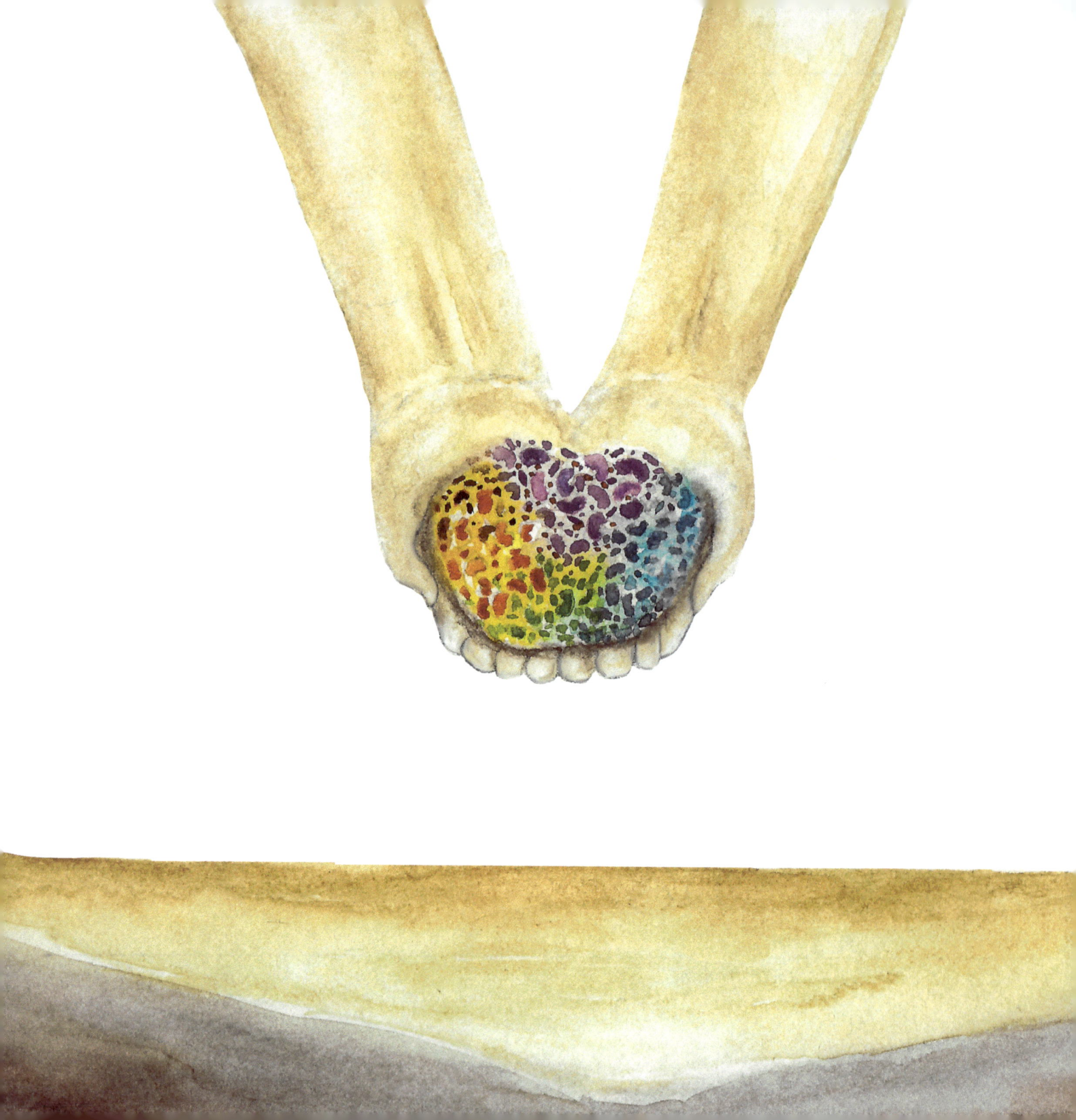

Sow
yourself
in
GOOD
SOIL,

...dear
GOOD
SEED!

Let the GARDEN within YOU,

GROW what you may need.

ALL

Mother Nature

wants

is
for your

SOUL

to

SUCCEED!

How to use this book

This is a companion book that is best used for daily simple meditations and writing I AM affirmations anywhere, indoors or in Nature.

Mindfully creating a daily habit of affirmations is a wonderful way of connecting to the positive voice within at a young age or any stage in life. It brings a positive feeling within and a wonderful sense of well-being.

Daily Affirmations

- Have your child SAY 5 - 10 or more 'I Am' affirmations in the morning upon waking up and/or at night before going to bed. Explain to your child your meaning of each affirmation attribute.

- Or have your child SAY 5 - 10 or more 'I Am' affirmations anytime while doing the simple meditation.

- Or have your child SAY 5 - 10 'I Am' affirmations anytime while doing a simple meditation. See the simple meditations in the next page.

Daily Writing Affirmations

- Also, you and your child can WRITE down 1-3 'I Am' Affirmations everyday

They can also explore writing these affirmation statements by combining two or more attributes.

Enjoy the wonderful habit of daily affirmations and meditations.

Simple Meditations

Close your eyes.
Put the palm of your hands on your heart.
Feel your heartbeat.
Breathe deeply.
Mind every breath.
Inhale and exhale at least 3 times.
Then say as many 'I Am' affirmations as you like.
Take your time.
When you are finished, you may open your eyes.

And smile.
Feel the gratitude in your heart.

I AM Affirmations

A

Absolute
Abundant
Accepting
Achieving
Accountable
Adept
Adequate
Adventurous
Amazing
Amiable
Appreciated
Appreciative
Assertive
Audacious
Authentic
Awakened
Awesome

B

Balanced
Beaming
Beautiful
Best
Bold
Blessed
Bright
Brilliant
Brave

E

Efficient
Empowered
Energetic
Encouraging
Enlightened
Enough
Enthusiastic
Epic
Exceptional
Excited
Expansive
Expert
Exquisite
Extraordinary

C

Calm
Capable
Caring
Champion
Charming
Cheerful
Clear
Clean
Cleansed
Clever
Compassionate
Complete
Comfortable
Committed
Communicative
Confident
Content
Cooperative
Correct
Courageous
Creative

D

Decisive
Deep
Delicious
Delightful
Dependable
Deserving
Determined
Diligent
Direct
Discerning
Divine

F

Fabulous
Faithful
Fascinating
Flamboyant
Flawless
Flexible
Flowing
Focused
Forgiving
Frank
Free
Friendly
Funny

G
Generous
Gentle
Glorious
Glowing
Graceful
Gracious
Grateful
Great
Gifted
Good
Growing

H
Happy
Harmonious
Healed
Healing
Healthy
Helpful
Honest
Honorable
Hopeful
Humble
Humorous

J
Jolly
Joyful
Joyous
Jubilant

I
Imaginative
Important
Inclusive
Independent
Indomitable
Industrious
Ingenious
Inspired
Inspiring
Intelligent
Intentional
Intuitive
Irresistible
Inventive
Invigorating

K
Keen
Kind
Kinesthetic

M
Magical
Magnanimous
Magnificent
Marvelous
Mindful
Minimalist
Mind-blowing
Miraculous
Modest

O
Obedient
One-of-a-kind
Open
Optimistic
Opulent
Orderly
Organized
Original
Outgoing
Outstanding

L
Light
Limitless
Love
Loving

N
Noble
Nurturing

P
Peaceful
Patient
Playful
Polite
Positive
Powerful
Precious
Present
Proactive
Productive
Proficient
Protective
Proud
Purified
Purposeful

I AM Affirmations

Q
Qualified
Quick
Quiet
Questioning

R
Radiant
Ready
Receptive
Recognized
Relaxed
Releasing
Reliable
Renewed
Resilient
Resolute
Respectable
Responsible
Right
Robust

S
Satisfied
Sensational
Serene
Significant
Simple
Sincere
Skillful
Smart
Soulful
Spectacular
Special
Splendid
Spiritual
Spontaneous
Strong
Successful
Sufficient
Sumptuous
Supportive
Steadfast
Sweet
Synergistic

T
Tactful
Tenacious
Tender
Terrific
Thankful
Thoughtful
Tolerant
Tranquil
Transformative
Trouper
Trustworthy
Truthful
Trusting

W
Warm
Wealthy
Well
Willing
Wise

U
Understanding
Unique
Uplifting
Unlimited
Unshakable

V
Valuable
Vibrant
Victorious
Vigilant
Visionary

Y
Youthful
Yearning

Z
Zany
Zealous
Zestful

About the Author

Apple (Chan) Resonance was born and raised in Manila, Philippines. She has been very passionate about art, design and vegetable gardening since childhood and even incorporated growing vegetables indoors in her graduate school project in 2003.

From Singapore, Apple moved to Los Angeles to continue practicing her Interior Design profession. However, she was redirected by the Universe into a calling of working with Nature and learning about guerilla gardening, seed-saving and organic edible gardening through SLOLA (Seed Library of Los Angeles). She began sustainably raising her family by growing their own food from seeds and living off of the land in their homestead in Topanga, CA, where Apple Nature-homeschooled her son for five years. She also started Lemongrass Press as a hobby from their homestead in 2016 after receiving countless messages from their garden to create gardening books for kids.

Apple was first introduced to the wisdom of the Findhorn Foundation through a seed artwork she was painting one sunny day after she gardened. Since then, she wanted to visit the Findhorn Foundation in 2017 and 2018 to see the Findhorn garden in person. And importantly, to get creative inspirations for this book's watercolor artwork. Finally, all stars aligned in the summer of 2019 and she was able to join the Experience Week at Cluny Hill and since then everything was a miracle unfolding.

For this book's watercolor artworks, Apple used Sennelier watercolor with sun-activated rain water, melted snow and lake water from Big Bear. Big Bear mountains could not be any more perfect. A tranquil place to be creative, be close to nature, be attuned and connected to oneself with daily sun gazing, prayers, meditations and affirmations.

Apple's favorite vegetables to grow from seeds are tomato, cucumber, turnip, zucchini, *ampalaya* (bitter melon), carrots, celery and rainbow chard.

Apple is also a wildlife conservation artist and contributor for ABUN (Artists and Biologists Unite for Nature) since 2019.

Apple's favorite affirmations are:

I am Love,

I am Light and

I am ONE with the Universe.

Books by Apple Resonance:

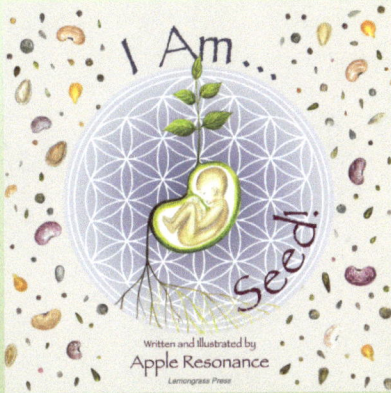

I Am Seed!

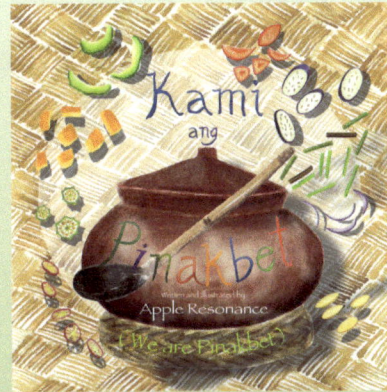

Kami Ang Pinakbet

More upcoming books by Apple Resonance:

I Am My Garden!

Every Child's Vegetable Gardening Journal

The Blue Baobab

The Street Sweeper

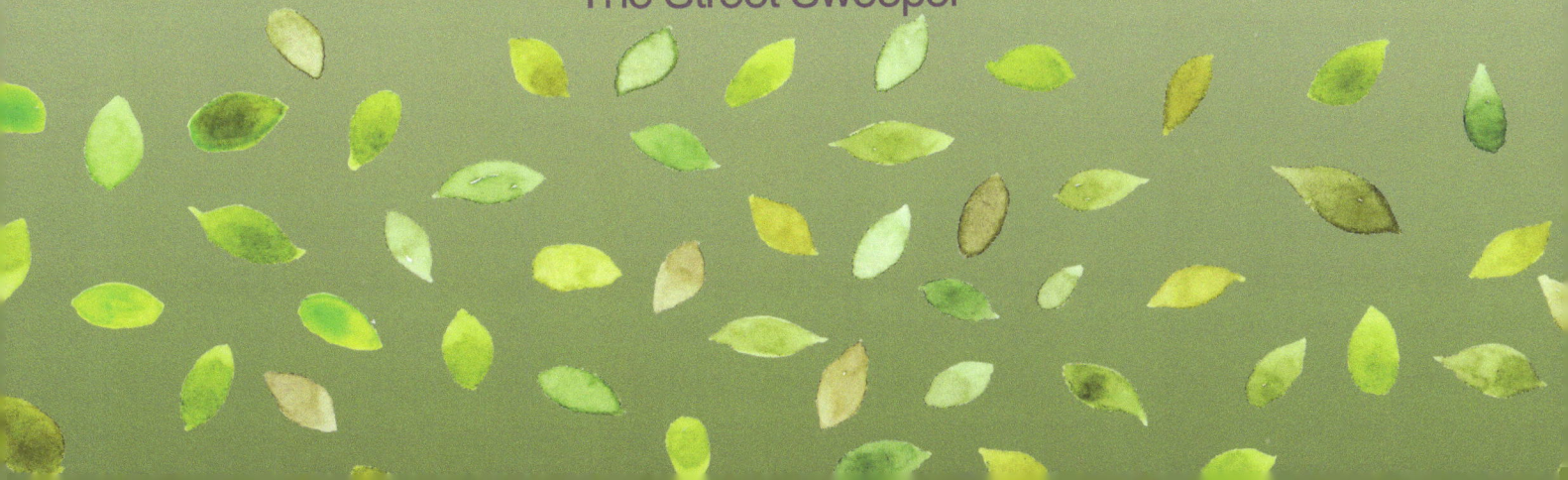

Who are **YOU**?

How well do you know yourself?

Every affirmation is like a **SEED** that you sow

and grow in your **BEING**.

You are who you believe to be.

You are who you decide to become.

You are who you create and re-create.

Into completion.

With authenticity.

www.ingramcontent.com/pod-product-compliance
Lightning Source LLC
Chambersburg PA
CBHW060849270326

41934CB00002B/60